IRISH FACTS

MEGHAN O'ROURKE

GRAMERCY BOOKS
NEW YORK

This 2000 edition is published by Gramercy Books™, an imprint of Random House Value Publishing, Inc., 201 East 50th Street, New York, N.Y. 10022.

Gramercy Books™ and design are trademarks of Random House Value Publishing, Inc.

Random House
New York • Toronto • London • Sydney • Auckland
http://www.randomhouse.com/

Cover design by Karen Ocker
Text design by Robert Yaffe

Front cover photos courtesy of Irish Tourist Board

Printed and bound in China.

Library of Congress Cataloging–in–Publication Data

    O'Rourke, Meghan.
      Fun Irish facts / Meghan O' Rourke.
        p. cm.
      ISBN 0-517-20805-9
      1. Ireland Miscellanea.   2. Irish Americans Miscellanea.
    I. Title.
    DA906.O76 2000
    909'.049162—dc21   99-43267
                                    CIP

8 7 6 5 4 3 2 1

CONTENTS

Books of similar interest from
Random House Value Publishing:

Ireland: A Photographic Tour
Irish Blessings
The Irish Spirit
Irish Wonders
Myths and Legends of Ireland
So You Think You're Irish
The Story of the Irish Race
A Touch of the Irish
A Treasury of Irish Myth, Legend, and Folklore
44 Irish Short Stories

The IRISH
AND THEIR ISLAND

The total area of Ireland (including Northern Ireland) is 32,595 square miles, slightly more than West Virginia.

The Irish coastline is more than 3,500 miles.

Ireland's highest mountain, at 3,414 feet, is Carrauntoohill.

The Shannon, Ireland's longest river, is 240 miles long.

Ireland's oldest bridge, built in the 9th century, was discovered near the village and monastery in Clonmacnoise in County Offaly. The 533-foot-long 17-foot-wide oak span over the Shannon River shows more skill and economic advancement than previously assumed.

Ireland's sunniest town is Rosslare in County Wexford, which has more than 1600 hours of sunshine per year.

According to recent statistics, the population of Ireland is estimated at 3.6 million. Approximately 43% of the population is under 25.

The greater Dublin Area accounts for more than 25% of the population of Ireland.

Current estimates put the Irish birth rate at 1.8 births per woman.

There are more than 70 million people worldwide who claim Irish ancestry.

Farm products contribute about 20% of the total value of exports. Livestock products represent more than 80% of the agricultural output.

Although fish are abundant in Irish waters, most fishing was controlled by foreigners, and until the 20th century there was no real fishing industry in Ireland. In addition to a more productive development of the industry, there are now fish farms—most along the western coast.

The bogs of Ireland cover some 10% of the island. Some bogs are as deep as 50 feet. Three million tons of turf from midland bogs is harvested annually as fuel for a quarter of Ireland's electricity. Another two million tons become briquets for home use and peat moss.

The stony land provided the materials for the monks of the Dark Ages to build their water-tight beehive huts—flat stone upon stone rising in ever smaller layers to the top where one large flat stone provided the roof. Many partial beehive huts remain on the Dingle Peninsula, in rocky pastures rising from the sea.

The basic Irish boat used in western Ireland and the islands is called the curagh. It is a high-riding craft that glides over the tops of waves. Made with a basket-like lath frame covered with hide or tarred canvas and rowed with two blade-less oars, the curragh can carry more than a ton of cattle, crops, pigs and passengers.

In Ireland, there are an estimated 250,000 archeological sites and antiquities.

Ogham stones served as gravestones in prehistoric times and the signs on them record the buried man's name. The ogham pillar stone at Ballycrovane, County Cork, is thought to be the tallest in Western Europe.

The areas of Gaeltacht, in Donegal, have the greatest numbers of people who speak Gaelic. Children from other parts of Ireland come to stay there to improve their Irish.

The area around Newtownards, County Down, is home to some of the world's most famous roses, including the "Grandpa Dickson" and "Iceberg."

On Achill Island, Ireland's largest, the word "boycott" got its beginnings. British Captain Boycott was so cruel to the peasants that they refused to work his lands, a tactic that was successful enough that the word "boycott" was created.

The Connemara ponies of today are descendants of ponies that arrived with the Celts. They can be traced to the original wild horses of the Ice Age, 20,000 years ago.

Blarney Castle, built in 1446, is the most visited castle in Ireland.

The Irish flag made its debut in 1848, a year of revolution. Its colors are green, white, and orange. The green represents the older Gaelic and Anglo-Norman population, while the orange represents the Protestant population, supporters of William of Orange. When Thomas Francis Meagher, its designer, introduced the flag, he said, "The white in the center signifies a lasting truce between the 'Orange' and the 'Green,' and I trust that beneath its folds the hands of the Irish Protestant and the Irish Catholic may be clasped in heroic brother-hood." It became the national flag in 1916.

The Soldier's Song was written in 1907 by Peadar Kearney, an uncle of Brendan Behan, was sung during the Easter Rising of 1916 and later at various camps where republicans were interned. Soon after, it was adopted as the national anthem, replacing *God Save Ireland*.

A portrait of Ireland's most famous poet, William Butler Yeats, appears on the Irish 10-pound note.

Approximately 95% of the residents of the Republic or Ireland are Catholic. However many Protestants played important roles in Ireland's quest for independence from Britain.

Ireland's largest church is St. Patrick's Cathedral in Dublin, which is 300 feet long. It is an Anglican church. St. Patrick's Cathedral in New York, a Catholic church, completed in 1879, is 306 feet long.

Ireland (Republic and Northern) has approximately 1,300 parishes served by about 4,000 priests. There are approximately 20,000 men and women in various religious orders of priests, brothers and nuns.

CUSTOMS AND
TRADITIONS

St. Patrick, the principal patron saint of Ireland, was not Irish. He was born in England and at the age of 16 was captured by Irish raiders and brought to Ireland as a slave. During this time he became deeply religious and began to have visions. Six years later he escaped to the Continent and settled in France. After having visions of bringing Christianity to the Irish people, he returned to Ireland in 432 A.D., and stayed there until his death.

Ireland's official color was originally blue, not green.

St. Brigid, as protectress of farming and livestock and one of Ireland's most important saints, was thought to be born in Faughart, County Louth in 453 A.D. It is believed that it was St. Patrick who baptized her.

Ireland's national animal is the horse.

The Harp, not the Shamrock, is the official emblem of Ireland.

In common with most of the world's music, the music of medieval Gaelic Ireland was non-literate. The harp was the dominant and characteristic instrument in historical times, and was adopted as the arms of Ireland in the 17th century.

The shamrock is undoubtedly the most identifiable symbol of Ireland. Shamrock comes from the Irish Gaelic word Seamrog, a word that refers to the plant's three leaves. Legend has it that during a religious debate with the Druid priests, St. Patrick plucked a shamrock to demonstrate the mysteries of the Christian Trinity—three leaves held together by a single stem. Whether or not this story is true, the shamrock is regarded as the national plant of Ireland and always worn on St. Patrick's Day.

Pampooties are traditional footwear made of untanned leather, still worn in the Aran Islands.

Murphy is the most common surname in Ireland.

Mac vs. Mc: There seems to be a belief that Mc is Irish and Mac is Scottish. There is no difference: Mc is simply an abbreviation of Mac.

The Gaels of Scotland are the descendants of the Gaelic settlers from Ireland. Scotland got its name from them, the word Scotus being Latin for Irishman.

Straw boys, wearing a cone-shaped or steeple hat of straw, used to appear on St. Brigid's Day and All Saints' Eve, and other occasions when "little folk" were out and about. Today, they are only seen in folk cultural gatherings.

The first three days of April are called "borrowed days" and are traditionally associated with bad weather.

Next to the dead, the Irish place a candle to give light, money to pay the fare over the river of death, and liquor to sustain the dead during the journey.

According to Irish tradition, at a wake, you sing a song and at a birth, you cry.

In Ireland, take three steps backward if you meet a funeral procession on a road.

For centuries it has been a practice in Irish villages to set the kitchen table after the evening meal on Christmas Eve. On it is a loaf of bread filled with caraway seeds and raisins, a pitcher of milk and a large lit candle. The door is left unlatched. Thus, hospitality is extended to the Holy Family or to any traveler who might be on the road.

The holly wreath, popular as a door decoration in North America, can be traced to early settlers from the south of

Ireland. Holly grows wild in the south of Ireland and at Christmas time houses are lavishly decorated with it.

The Celtic Christians had a practice called the "caim," in which they drew a circle around themselves. This was a symbol of the encircling love of God.

In Killorglin, County Kerry, the three-day summer festival in August, the Puck (Poc) Fair—which dates from 1613—gets off to a start when a large male goat (puck) is crowned King of the Fair.

Galway is the home of the International Oyster Festival, which features oyster-opening competitions and non-stop eating.

If a house was built during the period of a single day and a night, so that the smoke of a fire could be seen coming from the chimney at dawn the next day, then the occupants had won the right to live there. This custom was still practiced until comparatively recently in Ireland.

Many customs concerned the upkeep of the fireplace in a house. Apart from certain festival days, the fire was never allowed to go out. If it did go out it was considered an ill omen and a sign that the good luck of the house was being lost. To prevent the fire from going out, people had a way of settling the fire down at night so that it would remain

smoldering without burning away too much precious fuel. This was known as "smooring" the fire. Different parts of the country had their own chants and blessings which were recited as the smooring of the fire was carried out, to ask protection for the house, the hearth and the folk within.

It was traditional to leave ashes from the fireplace and all dirty water from the house outside before dark in order to avoid throwing any on the faeries who were out and about in the dark. In many places it was also the custom to leave gifts of milk and cheese outside the house for them.

Divorce has never been made legal in Ireland.

FAMOUS PEOPLE

Irish born poet Thomas Bracken wrote a poem in the 1870s that became the New Zealand anthem.

Robert Barton (county of Fermanagh) composed the tune of "Waltzing Matilda."

Samuel Beckett, born in Dublin in 1906, came from a Protestant Anglo-Irish family. His famous play, *Waiting for Godot*, was first performed in Paris. Beckett won the 1969 Nobel Prize for Literature.

Brendan Behan's autobiography *Borstal Boy* described his experiences in prison and his activities in the IRA.

Although Edmund Burke's biographers say that he was born in Dublin, it is now thought he was born in County Cork. He was educated at Quaker schools and Trinity College, Dublin. One of the foremost political thinkers of his time, his writings and powerful speeches are famous—and more popular today than when he delivered them.

Michael Collins, Irish patriot and soldier, was born in Clonakilty, County Cook, in 1890.

Father Edward J. Flanagan, born in Roscommon in 1886, founded Boys Town, U.S.A.

James Galway, world famous concert flutist, was born in County Antrim in Northern Ireland.

Sarsfield Gilmore, born in county Dublin in 1829, wrote the famous Civil War song, "When Johnny Came Marching Home."

Oliver Goldsmith, the son of an Irish clergyman, was born in County Longford in 1730. Trained as a physician, he was a prominent historian, novelist and playwright, whose work includes *The Vicar of Wakefield* and *She Stoops to Conquer*.

Arthur Guinness, founder of the Guinness Brewery, was born in 1725 in County Kildare.

Douglas Hyde, born in Roscommon in 1860, poet, playwright, and scholar, was the first president of the Gaelic League and became the first President of Ireland in 1937.

James Joyce was born in Dublin in 1882, the oldest of 13 children. He is best known a the author of *The Dubliners*, *A Portrait of the Artist As a Young Man* and *Ulysses*.

Lord Killanin, who lived in Galway, was president of the International Olympic Committee from 1972 to 1980. He also presided over the Connemary Pony Breeders and the Galway Race Track.

Catherine McAuley, founder of the Order of Mercy, the largest religious congregation in the English-speaking world, was born in Dublin in 1778.

Daniel O'Connell, considered a father of Ireland's freedom movement, was born in 1775 in County Kerry.

Michael O'Dwyer, patriot leader of the eighteen century uprisings, was transported to Australia where he became high constable of Sydney in 1815.

Thomas Parke (1857-1893) from County Leitrim, was a surgeon who accompanied Henry M. Stanley on his Congo explorations. He was credited with keeping the expedition from disaster.

Charles Stewart Parnell, champion of Home Rule in the late 1800s, was a native of County Wicklow.

Maureen O'Hara, star of *Jamaica Inn*, *How Green Was My Valley*, *Rio Grande*, and *The Quiet Man*, was born in Ranleigh, a suburb of Dublin in 1920. Born Maureen FitzSimons, her father was a clothier in Dublin and also owned part interest in a soccer team in Ireland called "Shamrock Rovers."

Mary Robinson was Ireland's first woman president. Born in Ballina, County Mayo, she was also the youngest professor of law ever at Trinity College in Dublin.

George Russell, known as A. E. Russell, was born in Lurgan, in Armagh County, in 1867. He was one of the founders of the Abbey Theatre.

George Bernard Shaw, who grew up in Dublin, received the Nobel Prize for Literature in 1925. Among his famous plays were *Arms and the Man*, *Man and Superman*, *Pygmalion*, and *St. Joan*.

John Millington Synge, was born in 1871 in Wicklow County. He lived in France and returned to Ireland to become a director of the Abbey Theatre in Dublin in 1904. His most famous play, *The Playboy of the Western World* was first performed in the Abbey Theatre in 1907.

Eamon de Valera, the first President of the Irish republic (1959-1973), was born in Brooklyn in 1882.

Ernest Walton, from Waterford, split the atom in 1931. He and his partner, John Cockcroft, received the 1951 Nobel Prize for Physics.

Oscar Wilde, the famous and flamboyant poet, playright, essayist, and critic, was born in Dublin in 1852. He described himself as "French by sympathy, I am Irish by race, and the English have condemned me to speak the language of Shakespeare." Wilde died in Paris in 1900.

Ireland's best known poet, William Butler Yeats, was born in 1865 in Dublin. His early career was as a playwright, and he founded the Irish Theatre, later the Abbey Theatre. He received the Nobel Prize for Literature in 1923. Perhaps his most famous poem is "The Lake Isle of Innisfree," set in his beloved ancestral home County Sligo, where he is buried.

tbe irisb
in america

The first St. Patrick's Day celebration in America was in 1737 in Boston.

In 1779, the first St. Patrick's Day Parade in New York was held. It was sponsored by the Volunteers of Ireland.

The first census of the United States, taken in 1790, recorded 44,000 Irish-born residents, more than half of them living south of Pennsylvania.

The most recent United States census revealed that more than 38 million Americans claim Irish ancestry. This is more than 9 times the total population of Ireland which totals approximately 3½ million.

As many as 25% of Americans claim pure Irish ancestry.

More than 40% of all United States presidents have claimed Irish ancestry.

Shamrock, Texas, also known as Irish City, U.S.A., is located in the Texas Panhandle. A piece of the original Blarney Stone was brought to Shamrock from Blarney Castle in County Cork and dedicated in 1959.

Commodore John Barry, born in 1745 in Wexford County, Ireland, was the founder of the United States Navy.

Billy the Kid, born Henry McCarty, was the son of Irish immigrants.

In 1775, Daniel Boone, descended from Donegal immigrants, accompanied by other pioneers of Irish origin, began the settlement of Kentucky.

U.S. Supreme Court Justice William J. Brennan, Jr. (1906-1997) was an Irish-American.

James Cagney, born in 1899 and raised on New York's Lower East Side by an Irish father and Norwegian mother, was best known for his roles as a tough gangster. He won an Oscar for his portrayal of Irish-American composer George M. Cohan in the 1942 film *Yankee Doodle Dandy*.

Charles Carroll III, born in Maryland in 1737, was the only Catholic to sign the Declaration of Independence.

Irish-American composer George M. Cohan, born in 1872, won a Congressional Medal for his World War I song "Over There" and also wrote "I'm a Yankee Doodle Dandy."

Irish-American Davy Crockett was born to a pioneer family in east Tennessee in 1786.

"Bing" Crosby appeared in more than 50 films, winning an Oscar in 1944 for *Going My Way* about a young Irish priest sent to serve a tough New York parish.

Richard Daley born in 1902, served six terms as mayor of Chicago.

Heavyweight champion Jack Dempsey was a descendant of Irish immigrants from County Kildare. The Manassa, Colorado-born Dempsey gained his title in 1919 and the nickname, "Manassa Mauler".

Sir Thomas Dongan, born in Kildare, was named Governor of New York in 1682. He held the post until 1688 and was subsequently named Earl of Limerick.

F. Scott Fitzgerald, novelist and author of *The Great Gatsby*, was born in St. Paul, Minnesota, in 1896. His mother, Mary McQuillan, was the daughter of a wealthy Irish immigrant.

John Ford, the father of Henry Ford, emigrated to America after being evicted from Cork in 1847.

Jackie Gleason, born in 1916 in Brooklyn, New York, was best known for his role as Ralph Kramden in *The Honeymooners*.

John Hancock, signer of the Declaration of Independence, traced his ancestry to Ulster.

An Irishman from County Kilkenny, James Hoban, designed the White House in 1792.

W. R. Grace, business leader and steamship line operator born in 1832, was the first Roman Catholic mayor of New York.

Helen Hayes, known as the first lady of the American theater was born in 1900. Among her stage credits were the title roles in *Mary of Scotland* and *Victoria Regina*. She also appeared in many films. She received the Medal of the City of New York and had a Broadway theater named for her.

 Irsh-American William Randolph Hearst (1863-1951) was born in San Francisco, the son of a self-made millionaire George Hearst. In 1887, he became proprietor of the San Francisco Examiner and during his career he built a publishing empire that included *The New York Morning Journal*, *The Chicago Examiner*, *The Boston American*, *Cosmopolitan* and *Harper's Bazaar*. His life inspired the Orson Welles film *Citizen Kane*.

John Joseph Hughes, a native of County Tyrone, came to America and worked on canals. In 1826 he was ordained and in 1842 became archbishop of New York.

Buster Keaton, born Joseph Francis Keaton in 1895 to Irish immigrants, was best known as a star of silent films.

Dancer and choreographer, Gene Kelly, born in Pennsylvania in 1928, starred in *Singin' in the Rain*, *On The Town*, and *An American In Paris*.

Grace Kelly (1928-1982), film and stage

actress whose parents came from County Mayo, won an Oscar for *The Country Girl*. She became Princess Grace of Monaco in 1956.

John Fitzgerald Kennedy, whose great-grandfather emigrated from County Wexford, was the first Roman Catholic to be president of the United States.

Joseph P. Kennedy (1888-1969) was born in East Boston and educated at Harvard. As a bank president, he amassed a fortune in the pre-Depression stock market. In 1937,

President Franklin Delano Roosevelt named him Ambassador to England, the first Irish Catholic to hold that position.

Connie Mack, one of baseball's greatest mangers, was born Cornelius McGillicudy in 1862 in Brookfield, Massachusetts. He changed his name so that it would fit into a box score.

John McCloskey, the first American cardinal of the Roman Catholic Church, was born in Brooklyn, New York, in 1810, the son of immigrants from County Derry.

 In 1784, Daniel McCormick, a native of Ireland and a director of the Bank of New York, was elected the first president of the Friendly Sons of St. Patrick, a fraternal organization.

Sandra Day O'Connor, born of Irish ancestry in 1930 was appointed the first female Supreme Court justice in 1981.

Carrol O'Connor, a native New Yorker, studied at the National University in Ireland before he began his acting career. He reached national fame portraying Archie Bunker in the televison series *All in the Family*.

Eugene O'Neil, the son of a popular 19th century Irish-American actor, was born in New York City in 1888. He won the Nobel Prize for Literature in 1936 and Pulitzer Prizes for four of his plays, including *Strange Interlude* and *Long Day's Journey Into Night*.

Irish-American Alfred E. Smith, born in 1873 on New York's Lower East Side, became Governor of New York and in 1928, won the Democratic presidential nomination. Anti-Catholic sentiment kept him out of the White House. Many years later, in 1960, Americans elected their first Irish-American Catholic president, John F. Kennedy.

ARTS AND
ENTERTAINMENT

The Irish harp, known in Gaelic as the *clairsearch* or *cruit*, has been played in Ireland since the 8th century. Originally, harps were carved from a single piece of wood and had metal strings played with the fingernails. Today's harps have gutstrings, which are played with fingertips like other string instruments. Irish legend credits the harp with magical powers.

Bagpipes arrived in Ireland in the late 15th century, and were played by the military and at funerals and sporting events.

The Uilleann Pipes, which originated in the 18th century (and are named for the Irish word for elbow), are perhaps the world's most sophisticated bagpipes. Unlike other bagpipes, a set of these includes bellows (inflate the pipes), drones (supply the bass, baritone and tenor), chanter (supplies the main melody in 2 octaves), and regulator (provides the chords).

It was an Irishman, John Fields (1782-1837), who created the nocturne form in music.

Handel's *Messiah* had its world premiere in Dublin in 1742.

The famous song, "It's a Long Way to Tipperary," was written in 1912 by Jack Judge, from Oldbury, near Birmingham, England, even though he had never visited Ireland. Allegedly, the song was first titled, "It's a Long Way to Connemara," but was changed to Tipperary because the county was better known.

Several of Ireland's famous writers—Oliver Goldsmith, Jonathan Swift, George Bernard Shaw, Oscar Wilde, Thomas Moore, and William Butler Yeats—were all Protestant.

 Ireland is known for its writers, poets, and playwrights. Among the most popular modern writers are: Maeve Binchy, Roddy Doyle, Frank McCourt, Frank O'Connor, Sean O'Faolain and Liam O'Flaherty.

The epic poem, *The Cattle Raid of Cooley*, is regarded as the Irish Iliad.

The Book of Kells, an ancient illustration of the Gospel, is over 1000 years old. It was created by Irish Monks.

Bram Stoker, the author of *Dracula*, was born in Dublin in 1847.

Jonathan Swift, author of *Gulliver's Travels* was known as a satirist, poet, and dean of St. Patrick's cathedral in Dublin. He suggested in his 1929 tongue-in-cheek essay, "A Modest Proposal," that the solution to Ireland's severe economic problems was the eating of young, healthy Irish children. He called them,  "a most delicious, nourishing and wholesome food, whether stewed, roasted, baked, or boiled, and I make no doubt that it will be equally served in a fricassee, or a ragout."

Thomas Moore, national poet of Ireland in the 18th century, wrote the words to many traditional Irish airs, such as "The Last Rose of Summer," and "Believe Me If All those Endearing Charms."

Frank O'Connor, the famous Irish playwright, novelist, and short story writer, was born in Cork in 1903.

Irish poet Seamus Heaney won the 1995 Nobel prize for literature.

 The film *My Left Foot* was based on the life of Irish writer-artist Christy Brown, who was born in Dublin with cerebral palsy.

William Butler Yeats, Edward Martyn, and Lady Gregory launched the Abbey Theatre in Dublin, which has become Ireland's National Theatre.

 Sean O'Casey's play, *The Plough and the Stars,* was presented for the first time at the Abbey Theater in Dublin in 1951. Its final act ends with the burning of Dublin. A few hours after the play ended, the theater was gutted by a fire.

Dublin's first movie theater, the Volta, was managed by James Joyce.

Siamsa Tire, the national folk theater of Ireland, is located in Tralee in County Kerry.

Liam Neeson, born in 1952 in Northern Ireland, originally planned a career as a teacher, attending Queens College in Belfast. In 1976, he joined the prestigious Lyric Player Theatre in Belfast and two years later joined the reperatory company of Dublin's Abbey Theatre. He has appeared in over twenty films including, *Excalibur*, *Shining Through*, *Nell*, *Rob Roy*, *Schindler's List*, *Michael Collins* and *Star Wars Episode 1.*

Because the Irish danced in fields, one old poem called dancing "tripping the sod."

The four types of Irish music and associated dances are the jig, set dances (performed to a specific tune that has remained set over time), reel, and hornpipe.

Some famous set dances include "Hurry the Jug," "Rub the Bag," "The Piper through the Meadow Straying," and "King of the Fairies."

Around 1750, Dance Masters began to travel through the country, stopping for about six weeks in a village, teaching Irish dancing in kitchens, farm outbuildings, crossroads, or hedge schools.

During the 1800s, the cake dance became popular. A cake was placed on a pedestal in a field, as prize for the winning dancer, who would "take the cake."

The world famous band, U2, with album sales in excess of 90 million, originated in Dublin.

SPORTS

Hurling, an ancient Irish sport that is like a very fast form of hockey, is considered to be the fastest field game in the world. Hurling is mentioned in the epic Irish poem, *The Cattle Raid of Cooley*, in which the hero, Cuchulain, is a wizard with the hurling stick, called the caman.

During the period of Brish Penal Laws (1695-1782), the Irish celebrated mass in secret and then held secret hurling matches between parishes, with up to 200 men on each side.

Road bowling is played in two counties, Cork and Armagh, where traffic is light. A course can be up to several miles long, with the winner crossing it in the fewest tosses. The ball is a 28 ounce "bullet" of solid cast iron. Roads run up and own grades, around bends, and sometimes across rail bridges and streams.

Soccer was introduced in Ireland in 1878 by John M. McAlery, a Belfast merchant, who had first seen it on his honeymoon in Edinburgh. In 1880, the Irish Football Association was established in Belfast.

Ireland played its first ever World Cup soccer qualifying match in 1934.

Ireland is one of a limited number of countries where rugby is a popular amateur sport.

Gaelic football is the most popular spectator sport in Ireland. It was developed as an alternative to soccer and rugby and contains elements of both.

Ireland's best-known flat race is the Irish Derby, held at the Curragh in Kildare in early summer. The Curragh is the headquarters of flat racing in Ireland and is also the home of Irish horse breeding and training.

The best known steeplechase race is the Irish Grand Nation, run at Fairyhouse Racecourse near Dublin during Easter Week.

The famous Tipperary foxhounds were originally bred by William Barton I in 1807.

Ireland's largest greyhound track is in Cork.

There are more than 250 golf courses throughout Ireland. The major Irish tournament on the international professional circuit is the Murphy's Irish Open.

Irish-American William Ben Hogan, born in Texas in 1912, was one of the most influential golfers of the 20th century. He won many major tournaments including the U.S. Open, British Open, Masters Tournament, and the PGA Championship.

Michael Carruth, from Dublin, won the Gold Medal in welterweight boxing in the 1992 Olympics. He was Ireland's first Olympic gold medalist in 36 years.

Boxer John L. Sullivan, was born in Boston in 1858. "The Boston Strong Boy" became an Irish-American sports hero. He was ultimately defeated by another Irish-American, Jim Corbett, the subject of the movie *Gentleman Jim*.

Dubliner Steve "The Celtic Warrior" Collins became the Irish world super-middleweight champion boxer in 1995.

The Royal Cork Yacht Club in Cobh, founded in 1720, is the world's oldest yacht club.

Irish-American Charles Comiskey, who had a professional baseball career with the St. Louis Browns, founded the Chicago White Sox in 1900. Comiskey Park baseball stadium carries his name.

LORE, LEGENDS, SUPERSTITIONS, AND SPELLS

Blarney Stone: Blarney means the gift of persuasive eloquence. Kissing the stone is supposed to bring this gift. One legend has it that an old woman cast a spell on the stone to award a king who had saved her from drowning. Kissing the stone while under the spell gave the King the ability to speak sweetly and convincingly.

Legend has it that St. Patrick pounded a drum and banished all the snakes from Ireland. There are no snakes in Ireland today.

 The Burren, Irish for "gray rocky place," is in County Clare. This eerie landscape is a natural rock garden, where plants native to the Arctic thrive next to subtropical flora. Beneath the scarred surface are spectacular caves and streams. Folk legends associated with the Burren say its holy wells can cure bad vision and its caves are home to ghostly horsemen. It is also reputed that mysterious lakes appear and disappear there, taking with them maidens who have been turned into swans.

Irish myth has it that horses have the ability to see ghosts.

It's said that the prophet Jeremiah fled Jerusalem and was shipwrecked on Ireland's shore where he was found by one Finn MacCool. Jeremiah taught him the Hebrew law of the Torah. Tara, site of the home of the High Kings on Devenish Island, is alleged to be derived from the word Torah.

 The leprechaun's greatest passion is making shoes. A leprechaun can always be found with a shoe in one hand and a hammer in the other.

Most leprechauns are ugly, stunted, broad and bulky. They possess all the earth's treasures but prefer to dress in a drab green coat. They smoke pipes called "dudeens" and they drink quite a bit of beer. Female leprechauns do not exist.

Near the Giant's Causeway in County Antrim was where the first legendary member of the O'Neill clan sailed toward Ulster in a contest in which the first one to land would claim the kingdom. O'Neill cut off his right hand and flung it onto the land—leading to the term, "the Red Hand of Ulster."

St. Brendan, Bishop of Clonfert, is said to have discovered America in 545 A.D.

Finn McCool, after whom the Fenians are named, was said to have lifted a rock out of Ulster and hurled it into the ocean, creating the Isle of Man. The hole left behind became a lake, the Lough Neigh.

According to legend, the Children of Lír were doomed to spend 300 years on three Irish lakes because their wicked step-mother turned them into swans. Swans on Irish lakes are still under the protection granted all swans by the grieving father.

The legendary "Lady Betty" had her death sentence commuted when she agreed to take on the unwanted job of Ireland's last hangwoman.

Lugh is the Celtic sun god and god of arts and crafts.

In Ireland, a mischievous fairy who often takes the form of a horse is called a pooka.

The best weapons against a fairy are fire and iron.

It's good luck to tear your wedding dress accidentally on your wedding day.

It is said that a dip in the River Shannon cures bashfulness and inhibition.

If a person turns his clothes inside-out at sunset, he will have good luck.

Tying a bag of clay around one's neck when going

to bed will promote the appearance of
one's future spouse in a dream.

Horses are considered lucky animals.
To allow horses to trample a little on
newly sown fields, would cause the seed to sprout well.

Among the many superstitions surrounding marriage, it was
thought that Monday and Friday were unlucky days for wed-
dings, the color green was unlucky and should not be worn
by the bride, and that if a glass or cup were broken on the
morning before the wedding it was an unlucky sign. Other
unlucky signs were the dropping of a wedding ring during
the ceremony or someone kissing the bride before the
groom did.

Charms and spells have been used in Ireland for centuries.
For safety when going on a journey, pluck ten blades of

yarrow, keep nine, and cast the tenth away for
tithe to the spirits. Put the nine blades in your
stocking, under the heel of the right foot and
the Evil One will have no power over you.

Rowan trees were planted just outside a house—or small pieces of rowan were placed on all the doorways and openings of the house—to ensure protection. The rowan was seen as a favorite of the fairies (the unseen beings of the otherworld) and so they would look kindly on places where the rowan could be found.

The seed of dock—a weedy plant of the buckwheat family —tied to the left arm of a woman will prevent her from being barren.

To tame a horse, whisper the Apostle's Creed in his right ear on a Friday, and again in his left on a Wednesday.
    Do this weekly until he is tame.

Everyone knows the shamrock is protection against bad luck, but so are holy water, goose grease and salt.

history

A burial ground near Carlow dates back to 6000 B.C. The Browne's Hill dolmen, marking the entrance, has a huge "capstone" on top of other stones. It is estimated to weigh over a hundred tons.

The largest Stone Age community was in Ceide Fields in County Mayo. It is believed that over 5,000 people lived there until 3000 B.C.

Archaeological evidence suggests that Achill Island was densely populated in 3000 B.C.

Celts came to Ireland about 600 B.C., and their culture persisted until the late 1500s.

In Celtic Ireland, around 200 B.C., no coins were used. The cow was the unit of exchange. The country was divided into about 150 miniature kingdoms, each called a "tuath."

In the 6th and 7th centuries A.D., Irish saints and monks spread Christianity to Britain and to western Europe, establishing monasteries and missions.

Irish monks sailed from Ireland and reached the Faeroe Islands off the Scandanavian coast in the mid-seventh century and settled in Iceland in the middle of the eighth century.

The Vikings invaded Ireland around 794 A.D. and founded the first towns, including Dublin. They were defeated by the Normans in 1170.

It is thought that an Irishman from Galway, William Eris (or Ayers) accompanied Columbus on his 1492 journey to America. He is said to have been one of the 40 volunteers left behind in Hispaniola who were killed by the Indians before Columbus's return.

Trinity College in Dublin was founded by Queen Elizabeth I in 1592.

The Scots have migrated to and from Ireland since ancient times, but the first modern Scottish settlement began in 1610.

When the English enacted the Penal Laws in the late 1600s banning the education of Catholic children, the Irish began hidden schools, called hedge schools. Traditional Irish culture was taught in secrecy.

Oliver Cromwell invaded Ireland in 1649. By 1656 over 60,000 Irish Catholics had been sent as slaves to Barbados and other islands in the Caribbean.

In 1672, over 6,000 Irish boys and women were sold as slaves to Jamaica, and then gained control over the island.

In 1680, George Talbot, an "Irish gentleman" received a land grant in Maryland, which he named New Ireland.

In 1688, Irish Catholics held 22% of the land in Ireland. By 1714, Catholics held only 7% of the land.

Orange culture began with the founding of the Orange Order in 1795 and it persists to this day.

In 1801, Ireland was made part of the United Kingdom.

Cobh, the Harbor of Cork, hosted the sailing of the first ocean-crossing steamer in 1838.

 The Irish potato blight occurred in 1845, causing a famine. By 1848, through emigration and deaths by famine, Ireland's population decreased by more than 2 million people.

By the 1840s, during the years of the famine, Ireland was exporting enough grain to Britain to feed two million a year. During the height of the famine, some of the parts of the country that were most stricken were exporting food to Britain. While people starved to death in Ireland, thousands of cattle were shipped to England.

In 1949, Ireland became an independent republic.

 Revival of Gaelic culture began around 1884, based largely on the culture of the Celts, but also on other Irish cultures and it persists to this day.

In 1916, the Irish Republic Brotherhood and the Irish Citizen Army staged the Easter Rebellion to protest British conscription of Irish into military service in World War I. The rebellion was crushed.

The Irish Republican Army (IRA) was formed in 1919 to fight for Ireland's independence from Britain.

Ireland—except for the 6 Ulster counties in Northern Ireland—became a Free State of the British Commonwealth in 1922.

In 1971, the first British soldier was killed by the IRA in Belfast.

LANGUAGE

The bodhran, from the word *bodhar* meaning dull-sounding or deaf, is a frame drum usually made of goatskin.

There are two languages, Irish Gaelic and English. Gaelic is spoken mainly in areas located along the western seaboard.

In spite of a 1937 constitutional decree proclaiming Gaelic the national language, those who speak Gaelic every day make up less than 1% of the population today.

Anam Cara in Gaelic means "Soul friend"—it is an ancient journey down a nearly forgotten path of wisdom into what it means to be human.

Whiskey comes from the Irish word, *uisce beatha* (pronounced ish-kuh-ba-ha), which means "the water of life."

The Celtic word "Belfast" means "approach to the sand spit" and until 1600 that is about all there was to Belfast— a wide spot in the river.

One word describing a brawl, *donnybrook*, comes from the name of a town in County Dublin.

The Irish slang word for mouth is *gab*, which explains the phrase "gift of the gab."

The name Dublin comes from the Irish *Dubh Linn*, which means Black Pool. Dublin's first name was *Eblana*, mentioned in 140 A.D. by the Macedonian Ptolemy.

Maguire comes from the Irish words *Mag Uidir*, meaning "son of the brown(-haired) one."

Merry Christmas in Gaelic is *Nolaig Shona*.

An expression of gratitude, "*Go mba seacht bhfearr a bheas tú bliain ó inniu*" means "May you be seven times better a year from today."

The root name of Ballymore, Ballina, and Ballinlough is *baile*, meaning town.

Cill, meaning church, is the root name for Killarney, Kildare Kilcullen, Kilkenny.

The root name for Derry, Londonderry, and all towns with "Derry" in their name is *daoire*, meaning oak wood or grove. Ireland used to have a great deal of woodland, but the British cut down the timber, in part to flush out rebels who lived in the forests.

Domhnach, meaning Sunday, or a church, is the root of Donnybrook, Donaghmore, and other towns with Donagh in their name.

The root name for Drumcree, and Dromahair is *droim*, meaning ridge or hillock.

Inis, meaning island or water meadow, is the root name for Ennis, Inch, and Lahinch.

The root of Lough, Loughbeg, and Loughrea is *loch*, meaning lake.

Sean, meaning old, is the root of Shandon, Shankill, and Shanmullagh.

ƒOOδ AΝδ δRIΝK

The potato is not native to Ireland. It was originally brought to Ireland from the Americas by Sir Walter Raleigh in 1585.

Beef, not beer, is Ireland's largest edible export.

Four million pints of Guinness beer are produced daily.

All the grain used by Guinness is grown in Ireland.

The Harp symbol on Guinness products is identical to the Irish government version except the Guinness version faces left and the official government version faces right.

Ireland's longest bar is the Grandstand Bar at Galway Race Course. It is 210 feet long.

Corned beef is not a traditional dish in Ireland, but it was popular with the Irish immigrants who settled in New York because it was 5 cents a portion, making it affordable.

A potato is sometimes called a Smiling Murphy.

Colcannon, a mashed potato dish made with kale, scallions, butter and hot cream or milk, is a Halloween specialty.

Boiled bacon and cabbage is considered Ireland's most popular traditional dish.

The traditional accompaniment to Christmas pudding is brandy butter.

Plum Cake, a famous Irish dessert, contains no plums. A traditional victorian plum cake includes dried fruit such as raisins, currants, and apricots, as well as candied orange and lemon, nuts, cinammon and molasses.

Traditional Irish toffee is called "yellow man."

Soda bread is one of Ireland's staple foods. Baked in a round loaf with a cross cut into the top, it easily divides into quarters or "farls."

Poteen, or poitin, named for the "little pot" in which it is normally made, is Ireland's version of moonshine—home-brewed liquor.

Drisheens, a County Cork specialty, are made by combining strained sheep's blood with milk, water, mutton suet, bread-crumbs and seasoning.

Another Cork specialty, crubeens, are made from pigs trotters or pigs feet.

Dublin Coddle is a meat stew, made primarily of Irish sausage, bacon, onions, and potatoes.

Approximately 50% of a bottle of Bailey's Irish Cream is fresh Irish dairy cream.

Worldwide consumption of Bailey's Irish Cream is 1,000 glasses a minute.

It is said that St. Comcille's (aka St. Columba) favorite dish was Brotchan Foltchep, a pottage made with leeks, butter, chicken stock, heavy cream and oats.

Boxty, a traditional meal from the northern counties of Ireland, is often served on Halloween. It is a form of potato cake.

Barm Brack is a round light fruit bread, dark from the combination of spices used to give the brack its special taste. It is traditionally served with tea after dinner or supper.

PROVERBS, SAYINGS
AND BLESSINGS

It's no use boiling your cabbage twice.

The cat likes fish, but does not like to wet her paws.

It is a bad wind that does not blow well for somebody.

He that does not tie a knot will lose his first stitch.

A constant guest is never welcome.

Death is a poor man's best physician.

He would go to mass every morning if holy water were whiskey.

A silent mouth is melodious.

A sweet voice does not injure the teeth.

A sweet tongue is seldom without a sting at its root.

Marry a woman out of the glen and you marry the whole glen.

A scholar's ink lasts longer than a martyr's blood.

Cattle are caught by their horns, people by their tongues.

You can't pluck a frog.

Wine drowns more men than blood.

"May your blessings outnumber the shamrocks that grow and may trouble avoid you wherever you go."

A wedding toast: "On this special day, our wish to you, the goodness of the old, the best of the new. God bless you both who drink this mead, may it always fill your every need."

Another wedding toast:
"Here's to the home that (insert bride and groom's names) shall build:
It shall have a kitchen on the first floor,
A bar on the second floor,
A bedroom on the third floor,
And a cathedral on the fourth.
So they can eat when they are hungry,
Drink when they are dry,
Make love when they are lonely,
And have salvation when they die."

God needed laughter in the world,
So he made the Irish race,
For they can meet life with a smile
And turn a happy face.

May your days be as bright
As the lakes of Killarney,
Your spirits be high
As the blue Irish sky,
May you walk in the path
Where the shamrocks are growin'
And blessings to you
For a wonderful day!

May you be half an hour in Heaven
Before the Devil knows you're dead.

May the hinges of our friendship never grow rusty.

May the lilt of Irish laughter
Lighten every load,
May the mist of Irish magic
Shorten every road,
May you taste the sweetest pleasures
That fortune ere bestowed,
And may all your friends remember
All the favors you are owed.

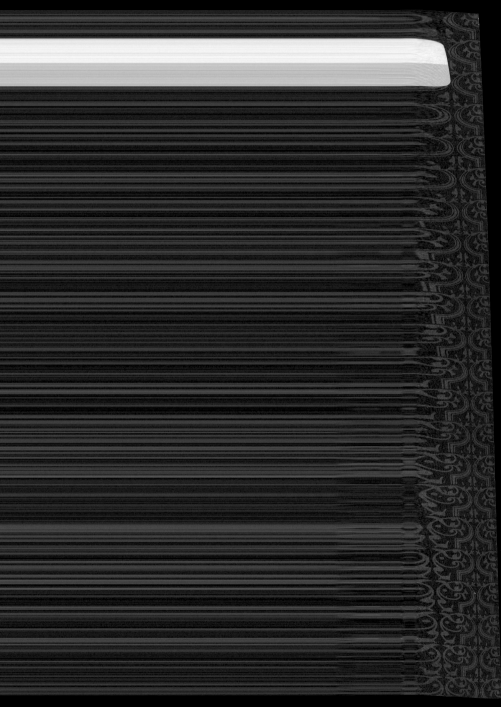